Popcorn

The Great Fire of London

Jenny Powell

WAYLAND

Explore the world with **Popcorn** – your complete first non-fiction library.

Look out for more titles in the **Popcorn** range. All books have the same format of simple text and striking images. Text is carefully matched to the pictures to help readers to identify and understand key vocabulary.
www.waylandbooks.co.uk/popcorn

First published in 2009 by Wayland

Copyright © Wayland 2009

Wayland
Hachette Children's Books
338 Euston Road
London NW1 3BH

Wayland Australia
Level 17/207 Kent Street
Sydney NSW 2000

Editor: Katie Powell
Designer: Phipps Design

British Library Cataloguing in Publication Data
    Powell, Jenny
    The Great Fire of London. - (Popcorn. History corner)
    1. Great Fire, London, England, 1666 - Juvenile literature
    I. Title
    942.1'2066

ISBN: 978 0 7502 5773 2

Printed and bound in China

Wayland is a division of Hachette Children's Books,
an Hachette UK company.
www.hachette.co.uk

Photographs:
Bettmann/Corbis: 14, Mary Evans Picture Library: 12, 16, 18, 19, The Gallery Collection/Corbis: 4-5, John Hayls/Getty Images: 15, Illustrated by Donald Herley/B.L. Herley Ltd: 2, 7, 17, Justin Kase zfivez/Alamy: 20-21, Private Collection/Bridgeman Art Library, London: 11, Private Collection/© Look & Learn/Bridgeman Art Library, London: Titlepage, 10, Time & Life Pictures/Getty Images: 6, Time & Life Pictures/Mansell/Getty Images: COVER, 8-9, © 2006 Charles Walker/TopFoto/TopFoto.co.uk: 13

 Contents

London in 1666

London is the capital city of England. In 1666, more than 500,000 people lived there.

In that same year, a fire destroyed many buildings in London. It was called The Great Fire of London.

This what London looked like before the fire.

Where it all began

The Great Fire of London began on
2nd September 1666. It started at
Tom Farryner's bakery on Pudding Lane.

Tom Farryner's bakery might have looked like this.

Tom Farryner was the baker for King Charles II and cooked for the royal court.

The fire started when hot coal
fell out of the oven. The fire spread
quickly over the straw on the floor.
Pudding Lane was soon in flames.

 # London's burning!

By the next day the fire had
spread from street to street.

In **1666**, buildings in London were built close together and made from wood. Wood burns quickly, so the fire soon spread across the city.

Fighting the fire

Huge flames destroyed London Bridge, and more than 300 homes burned down.

Water squirts were used to fight the flames.

People sheltered from the flames in stone buildings because these did not catch fire so easily.

There were no fire engines. Men had to use buckets of water and water squirts to put out the fire.

Lines of men passed buckets of water to throw on the fire.

The king in charge

King Charles II took action after St Paul's Cathedral burnt down. He ordered buildings to be pulled down to stop the fire spreading.

When St. Paul's cathedral caught fire, it quickly crumbled to the ground.

Many people fled from the flames.
The king tried to encourage men
to stay and help by giving them money.

Some people escaped in boats along the River Thames.

The fire dies out

Eventually the flames began to die down
and the fire was finally under control.

After the Great Fire, London was in ruins.

A man called Samuel Pepys
wrote about the fire in his diary.
It is still used today to find out
about London in 1666.

Pepys buried some
Parmesan cheese
and wine in his
garden to keep
them safe from
the fire.

What damage was done?

The fire burned for four days. Fewer than 10 people died but thousands of people were made homeless.

Many buildings were damaged during the fire.

More than 13,000 houses burned down,
and many hospitals and churches.

This is how London looked before the fire.

You can see how much damage was caused by the fire.

A new London

After the fire, the city had to be rebuilt.
The architect Sir Christopher Wren,
designed the new city of London.

Sir Christopher showed his plans to the king.

New rules were made about buildings. They had to be built from stone and set further apart. Later on, fire engines were also introduced.

The first fire engines were pulled by horses.

London today

In 1677, a tower called The Monument was built. It helps us to always remember the Great Fire of London.

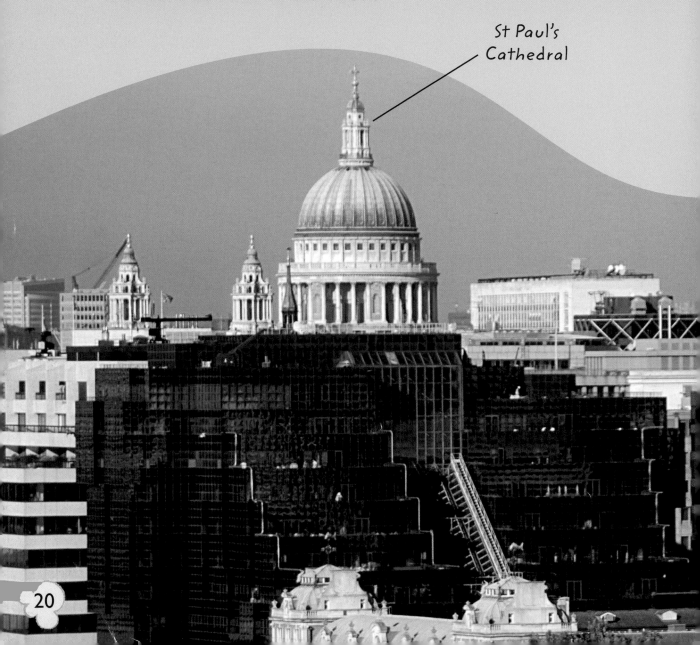

St Paul's Cathedral

London is still being built and rebuilt today. It is one of the most famous cities in the world.

The Monument

Make your own diary

Follow these simple steps to make your own 'Great Fire of London' diary, just like Samuel Pepys.

You will need:
- 1 tsp of coffee granules
- 1 piece of white A4 paper
- some paper towel
- some water • a cup
- a pencil

1. Put the coffee granules into a cup. Add some warm water from the tap.

2. Dip the paper towel into the coffee mixture and wipe it over the paper.

3. Wait for the paper to dry. Tear off the edges of the paper to make your diary look old.

4. Begin writing your own diary entry. Don't forget to add the date!

Great Fire of London
DIARY

3rd September, 1666

Fire safety tips

- Never play with matches, candles, fireworks or lighters.

- If you get burnt by touching a hot object or liquid, run the area under the tap with cool water for 3–5 minutes. Tell a grown-up about the burn.

- Do not leave clothes or toys near a fire or a heater.

- Ask an adult to fit smoke alarms in each room in your home and check they work properly.

- Make sure everyone in your home knows how to escape in a fire.

- If you think there might be a fire get out of the building quickly and calmly. **Dial 999.**

23

Glossary

architect
someone who
designs buildings

bakery
a shop which
makes bread, pies,
pastries, cakes,
biscuits and cookies

Capital city
the main city
where the country's
government meets

cathedral
the main church
in a city

diary
a book where people
record events

London Bridge
a bridge over the River
Thames in London

oven
a machine used for
cooking, heating, baking
or drying

rebuild
to repair something
and make it stronger

River Thames
the river that flows
through London

water squirts
an early kind of
water hose used
to fight the fire

Index

KE	06/04